Hercules and the Birds and Other Poems

Sangharakshita

For thirty years Sangharakshita has been playing an important part in the spread of Buddhism throughout the modern world. He is head of the Western Buddhist Order (Trailokya Bauddha Mahasangha), and is actively engaged in what is now an international Buddhist movement with centres in thirteen countries worldwide. When not visiting centres he is based at a community in Norfolk. His writings are available in eleven languages.

Also by Sangharakshita:
Messengers from Tibet and Other Poems
A Survey of Buddhism
Flame in Darkness
The Enchanted Heart
The Three Jewels
The Essence of Zen
Crossing the Stream
The Path of the Inner Life
The Thousand-Petalled Lotus
Human Enlightenment
The Religion of Art
The Ten Pillars of Buddhism
The Eternal Legacy
Travel Letters
Alternative Traditions
Conquering New Worlds
Ambedkar and Buddhism
The History of My Going for Refuge
The Taste of Freedom
New Currents in Western Buddhism
A Guide to the Buddhist Path
Learning to Walk

The Meaning of Orthodoxy in Buddhism
Mind—Reactive and Creative
Aspects of Buddhist Morality
Buddhism and Blasphemy
Buddhism, World Peace, and Nuclear War
The Bodhisattva: Evolution and Self-Transcendence
The Glory of the Literary World
Going For Refuge
The Caves of Bhaja
My Relation to the Order

Hercules and the Birds
and Other Poems

Sangharakshita

Windhorse Publications

Published by Windhorse Publications
136 Renfield Street
Glasgow G2 3AU

© Windhorse Publications 1990

Cover design Dhammarati

Printed by F. Crowe & Sons, Norwich

British Library Cataloguing in Publication data
    Sangharakshita, Bhikshu, Sthavira, 1925—
    Hercules and the Birds and Other Poems
    I. Title
    823.914

ISBN 0-904766-43-8

Table of Contents

Hercules and the Birds

I

Pink and white upon the hillside
Down in Naples, stands the massive
Archaeological Museum.
Palm trees stand before its portals,—
Date palms, crowned with feathery branches,—
While all round it, never ceasing,
Roars and howls and shrieks the traffic.
Silent in the lofty galleries
Stand or sit the white Immortals,
With the Heroes and the Roman
Emporers, naked or be-toga'd—
Stand or sit in bronze and marble,
Sad remains of ancient greatness.
Some, alas, are headless, armless,
Some, alas, are cracked and broken,
Or disfigured by the vandal.
There, majestic, stands Athené,
But her hand is Victory-less;
There the wise and bright Apollo,
But his bow and lyre are broken
(Headless, buxom Aphrodité
Shameless shows a shapely bottom).
Yet, within those lofty galleries,

One, at least, stands whole and perfect,
Clean as from the sculptor's chisel;
One, at least, shows undiminished
All the living faith of Hellas.
He, the greatest of the Heroes,
He, the Herculés Farnesé,
By the undelved earth protected
Centuries long, and resurrected
To the wondering gaze of mortals
At the height of the Renáissance
Stands there, looking down gigantic
On this modern world of pygmies.

II

Later, back at Il Convento,
At my desk before the window,
Taking up the picture postcard
That I bought in the Museum,
Long I gaze at the completeness
Of the Herculés Farnesé.
Brawny thighs and massive torso,
Shoulders broader than a barn-door,
Small head, curly-haired, based solid
On a bull-like neck half hidden
By a beard that falls lúxuriant
To a chest of amplest measure—
Thus I see him. He is leaning
On a club of knotted olive,
That head downwards he is resting
On a round and rugged boulder.

On the club is draped a lion-skin,—
Lion-skin many-folded, ample,—
While beneath the Hero's dangled
Left arm, with its hand half-curving,
Hangs the lion-head, jaws disparted.
Stern but gentle he is leaning
On his club of knotted olive,
Thoughtfully his brow inclining,
Resting from his mighty labours.
Simple and sublime he stands there,
Less than god, but more than mortal.
He has slain the lion Neméan,
Wears its pelt now for a garment.
He has slain the marsh-born Hydra,
Crushing with his club the monster's
Multiplying heads, and dipped his
Arrows in the poisonous blood-gouts.
He has caught alive the magic
Brazen-hoofed and golden-antlered
Cerynthéian Hind, the fleet one:
Over hill and dale he chased her
One whole year; then caught and bound her.
He has caught alive the monstrous
Erymánthian Boar, the fierce one;
Chained him, foaming, in a snow-drift.
He has cleansed the Aúgean Stables,
Where three thousand head of cattle
Thirty years and more had sheltered;
Cleansed them in a day, diverting
Through their doors a mighty river.
He has chased away the Harpies,

Foul defilers of the banquet;
Chased away the noisome Bird-things,
Woman-headed, with his arrows.
He has caught alive the Cretan
Bull, the fiery-breathed, the white one;
Caught the Minotaur's begetter.
He has from the Thracian uplands
Stolen Diomedés' Horses;
Horses that their cruel master
Fed on human flesh each morning.
He has reft the Golden Girdle
From the breasts of Hippolyté,
But, alas! has slain the maiden
In her Amazonian fierceness.
He has sailed towards the sunset,
To an island in the Ocean
Where the Sphinx's monstrous father
And the progeny of Arés
Guard the Oxen of Gerýon:
With his club he overcame them
And possessed him of the cattle.
He has brought the Golden Apples
From the ever-blooming Garden;
Golden apples dragon-warded
While the white-robed maidens, singing,
Circled round the sacred branches.
He has into Hell descended,
Dragged the triple-headed Guardian
Of the Gates of Hell, protesting,
Up into the light of Heaven.
Many other mighty labours

He, unceasing, has accomplished;
Labours for the good of others
And himself to purify
From pollution of kin-murder:
(Driven mad by jealous Hera,
Queen of Heaven, he, unwitting,
Took the lives of sons and nephews).
All the monstrous births of Nature,
Misbegotten, slime-engendered,
He has wholly extirpated;
All their foully-nurtured children
He has either slain or shackled.
Tyrants from their thrones deposing,
Succouring the weak and helpless,
Law and justice like twin pillars
He has planted in the kingdoms.
Now, deep-brooding, he is resting,
Resting from his mighty labours—
He, the greatest of the Heroes,
He, the Herculés Farnesé.
There, within those lofty galleries,
Leaning on his club of knotted
Olive draped with pelt Neméan,
He is standing, whole and perfect.
Laying down the picture postcard
That I bought in the Museum
Long I dream of his completeness.

III

Sudden, from beneath my window,
Comes a sound of shouting, barking.
Looking out, I see below me
Men and dogs from Fiats tumbling.
All the men are armed with rifles,
All are dressed in olive denim;
All upon their heads are wearing
Shooting-caps with little feathers,
While from bulging jacket pockets
Necks of bottles are protruding.
On the slope they stand consulting,
Loading rifles, slamming car doors,
Then with dogs behind them frisking
Scatter out across the hillside
As, above the dying hubbub,
From the church across the valley
Clangs the Sunday early Mass bell.
Soon, from deep within the foothills,—
Tuscan foothills, forest-mantled,—
We can hear the crack of rifles,
As the modern race of heroes
There pursue their week-end labours.
Later, on our walks we meet them
Skulking in the rock-strewn by-paths,
Crouching underneath the bushes,
With their rifles at the ready
And their fingers on the trigger.
Some are camouflaged with branches,
Some have decoy-birds in cages;

Others, from their hide-outs, blow on
Decoy-whistles, sweetly warbling
(Every now and then a bottle
Raising to their lips and swigging).
Year by year they come, remorseless,
In the pleasant Tuscan Autumn,
When the olive-fruits are gleaming
Black among the grey-green foliage,
And, beside the stony pathway,
Cyclamens, the pink and frail ones,
Push up through the rotting leafmould
And the withered leaves and grasses.
They have slain the chirping sparrows,
Slain the linnet and the whitethroat,
Slain the robin and the wagtail,
Slain the magpie and the pigeon,
Slain them in their tens of thousands,
Till within those ancient foothills,—
Tuscan foothills, forest-mantled,
Ever green, and aromatic,—
Rarely now are heard the songbirds
Fluting from the leafy branches;
Rarely, rarely, do we see them
Flitting to and fro like shadows
On the outskirts of the forest.
Yet, though year by year the hunters
Farther have to range and wider
(As the birds, their numbers dwindling,
Deeper shrink within the coverts),
Still, on pale blue Autumn evenings,
Off they go with dogs and rifles;

Still, on deep blue Autumn evenings,
Back they come with bulging game bags:
While, throughout the gold-blue Autumn
Day, from deep within the foothills,
Comes the hateful crack of rifles
As the modern race of heroes
Go about their week-end labours.

IV

Last night in a dream I saw him,
He, the greatest of the Heroes,
He, the Herculés Farnesé,
Less than god, but more than mortal.
Like a solitary mountain
That, upon the far horizon,
In some long untrodden region
Looms above a barren landscape;—
Like a thundercloud that, swollen,
Rolls up from the heaving ocean
And, above the earth impending,
Threatens to discharge its burden;—
Like the smoke of a volcano,
That, in mighty volumes towering,
Spreads across the face of heaven,
While, within the parent crater,
Bubbles up the yellow lava;—
Like a forest fire that, raging,
Roars and crackles through the woodland,
Licking up the trees and bushes
With its tongues of gold and scarlet—

Thus I saw him. From his shoulders
Hung the skin of lion Neméan,—
Lion-skin many-folded, ample,—
With the mighty forepaws, knotted,
Crossed upon his naked bosom,
While above his head the massive
Lion-head, like a crested helmet
Resting, reared itself, triumphant.
Whirling high his club of knotted
Olive, that athwart the landscape
Cast a black and dreadful shadow,
He with giant step was striding
Ridge to ridge across the foothills.
As he went, he drove before him
All the men with dogs and rifles,
All the modern race of heroes:
Like a flock of sheep he drove them.
With his foot the weapons crushing,
With his hand the decoys freeing,
On he strode—the birds around him
Fluttering cloudlike, loudly singing.
Birds upon his head and shoulders,
Birds upon his beard and lion-skin;
Birds upon his club of knotted
Olive perching in their thousands—
On I saw him moving:—saw him
Pass from land to land, redressing
All the wrongs that on the weaker
By the stronger are inflicted,
And, within the souls of millions,
Sow the dragon seed of vengeance;

Saw him drive before him, headlong,
All the brood of fraud and rapine,
All the hosts of lust and violence,
All the forces of destruction;
Saw him crush the robot armies;
Saw him smash the hideous weapons;
Saw him from their sunless prisons
Free the victims of oppression;
Saw him cleanse the earth and ocean;
Saw him build anew the cities;
Saw him forge between the nations
Golden links of truth and friendship,
Ever-during.—*Thus* I saw him
Last night in my dream or vision,
He, the greatest of the Heroes,
He, the Herculés Farnesé,
Bent on ever-nobler labours
For the good of others;—saw him—
Sun of Justice—in the heavens
Blazing; saw him golden, glorious,
Showering beams of blessing;—saw him
Show how strength, by love directed,
Shapes anew this world of mortals,
And, upon a nobler pattern,
Rears our heavenly-earthly city;
Till, from mortal to Immortal
Changing, after many labours'
We, like him, to high Olympus
Raised, from Hebé's rosy fingers
Receive at last the cup ambrosial.

Poems on Paintings from the 'Genius of Venice' Exhibition at the Royal Academy

1. Prologue

(With acknowledgements to A.E. Housman)

Noblest of schools, the Royal today
Is hung with paintings grave and gay,
And rises mid the streets and mews
Clad in a thousand wondrous hues.

Now, of my threescore years and ten,
Sixty will not come again,
And take from seventy years three-score,
It only leaves me ten years more.

And since for seeing works of grace
Ten years is but a little space,
This morning I must go, it seems,
To see the Royal hung with dreams.

2. Tobias and the Angel

(After the painting by Savoldo)

He sits at ease upon the rocks,
The Angel with the outspread wings;
Loosely to limbs of noblest mould
His rose and silver vesture clings.

Watchful he sits, right arm half raised
In monitory gesture sweet,
While travel-worn the small grey dog
Sleeps darkling near his naked feet.

Caught by that gesture as he kneels
Tobias turns, as in a dream;
Knowing his destined hour is come
The great fish gapes from out the stream.

3. The Temptation of St Anthony

(After the painting by Veronese)

Again with hideous thud the club descends,
Wielded by naked devil's brawny arm,
As, sprawling on his back, the red-robed saint
Clutches the book that wards off ultimate harm.

Behind his grizzled head, her bosom bare
Save for light gauze, a female devil bland
And beautiful, bright hair in snaky wreaths,
Scratches with coal-black claws his upraised hand.

4. Salome

(After the painting by Titian)

With looks demure, and tress that down her cheek
Straggles, enhancing every ripening charm,
She holds the Baptist's head upon a dish
And feels his hair upon her naked arm.

5. The Adoration of The Magi

(After the painting by Schiavone)

Heretics roasted for the love of Christ
Can things inanimate indeed foresee?
Between the Magi and the holy Child
The giant pillar writhes in agony.

Fluttering above, a half-clad angel bears
Both crown and wreath on this tumultuous morn.
Oh turn him back! Oh bid the horsemen go!
Better that Mary's Son had ne'er been born.

6. The Lion of St Mark

(After the painting by Carpaccio)

Behold the Lion of St Mark!
His steps are on both land and sea;
Proudly he wears his eagle wings,
For power is his, and victory.

Opened before him is the Book
In which are written, black and bold,
Those words which to the Most Serene
Like thunder down the ages rolled.

Beneath his wings the galleons ride;
Before his face rise dome and tower,
Together with that sumptuous pile
In which three architectures flower.

In aureoled glory self-absorbed,
And fangs half-bared, he does not see
The beauty of the humble shrubs
That clothe with life the sandy lea;

He does not see the lowly weeds
That pave the ground, and still will pave,
When all the pomp of Venice lies
Beneath the green and gilded wave.

Padmaloka

Three Summers and three Autumns have I seen,
And two white Winters, in this quiet spot,
And now the gold shines out among the green,
And reddest roses are remembered not.
For the third time are Winter's icy fingers
Stretched out—and yet the latest sunflower lingers.

Three Summers and three Autumns! In that time
I have made friends with walnut and with oak,
Have clasped the trunks of holly and of lime,
And cómmuned with them, though no words we spoke.
Watching black ants among the roots of grasses
I heard the wind sigh how our pleasure passes.

Russet and gold, the drifts of leaves are deep,
And the third Winter deep will be the snow;
But the trees mourn not, though no sap may leap,
For deeper still the gnarled roots thrust below.
In this quiet spot, girt by the reeds and rushes,
The soul roots deeper, and the spirit hushes.

Summer and Autumn, on the margined pond,
The waterlily's leaves are broad and green,

Soon to be yellowed, with the shrubs beyond,
And underneath a film of ice be seen.
But come first Spring, among her budding daughters
Red blooms the lily on the sunlit waters.

Dreaming and thinking as the Autumn ends,
I like the swallow must prepare for flight,
Must leave deep-rooted here my ancient friends
And go where night is day, and day is night.
Brief though my stay, I shall be thinking ever
Of this quiet spot, beside the sluggish river.

Thinking and dreaming, in this quiet spot,
Summer and Winter, I shall end my days,
Till like the rose I am remembered not,
And life has vanished with the sunset-rays.
Then, among silver lakes and golden mountains,
The new-born lotus smiles beside the crystal fountains.

Tuscany 1983

Between the tree-clad hills the misty plain,
Beyond the misty plain the sea—
A silver-shining ribbon void of stain;
Above, the sky's immensity
Intensely blue, and at the zenith bluest,
As truth within the faithful heart is truest.

On the hill opposite an ancient town
Dreaming, compáct of houses white,
Red-roofed, green-shuttered, some half tumbling down,
With yellow clock-tower shining bright
In th' evening sun, and telling every hour
How time holds all things mortal in its power.

On *this* hill, deepening silence all the day
Inside the convent's crumbling walls;
Through the gloom slanting, many a golden ray
Lights dusty corridors and falls
On red uneven pavements where, long since,
Shuffled cowled monk, strolled courtier, and strode prince.

Below us, at the bottom of the hill,
Beneath black cypresses the dead
Are quiet in tombs, but we are quieter still
In cloisters long untenantéd,
Learning what to be and not to be
Between the olive harvest and the sea.

Greenstone

High in the mountains, up creeks,
Between slopes densely tree-covered,
In the beds of ancient streams,
Stand the boulders.

Split them open,
And they are pure green—
Spinach green, apple green, and sea green.

The Maoris
Carved neck-amulets
And gleaming translucent fish-hooks
Out of the pure greenstone,
And polished batons
For great personages to hold
On ceremonial occasions.

Tourists
Can buy it made into ashtrays,
Lampstands, and little boxes.

What a pity!

Sonnet

Among the mighty mountains sojourning,
Years and decades went by as I beheld
Peak after peak at dawn or evening
Flushed with a golden glory that compelled
An ultimate homage as the day upwelled
Or night descended. Thrones of gods they seemed,
Those dazzling virgin snow-peaks—gods who dreamed
Immortal lives away, by time unknelled.

But now, as in a dream myself, I see
The bare and level fields stretch far away:
Nothing but light and space the scene affords.
Through th' green, a ground of lapis lazuli
Shines deepest blue, and hedges, brown and grey,
Turn to a net of glittering golden cords.

Lines Written for the Dedication of the Shrine and the Opening of The London Buddhist Centre at 'Sukhavati'

Flanked by the lotus red
The Buddha's golden head
And golden body on the altar gleam.
The white-robed worshippers
And red-stoled servitors
In through the open doorway joyful stream.
A thousand days of labour done,
Glad faces, as they sit there, catch the evening sun.

In through the windows wide
The slanting sunbeams glide,
Setting on each bowed head a crown of flame,
As from a thousand throats
Chanted are sweetest notes
Praising the Buddha's, Dharma's, Sangha's name.
The sound of tinkling silver bells
And long-reverberant gongs the mighty chorus swells.

On this triumphal day
With gods and men we say:
Long by the Buddha may the lotus red
Bloom and rebloom! Oh long
May we uplift our song,
Bringing light to the blind, life to the dead!
From this gold Presence, day and night,
Long may there shine on all, undimmed, the Infinite Light!

Lines to Jayapushpa on her Return to Malaysia

Dear daughter of a tropic isle,
For twice twelve months your radiant smile
Has blessed our dreary London streets,
Whereon the rain remorseless beats,
And where the sun is rarely seen
Gilding grey roofs and treetops green.
You stayed with us to learn anew
The song that had enraptured you
In your green paradise, but which
Had fallen from its proper pitch,
And having learned, you sang as clear
And sweet as some who'd practised here
For many a month and many a year.
But now that your two years are flown,
When you have won all hearts, and grown
For radiant smiles and sweetest song
One of the dearest of our throng,
You must return to your own groves,
To brighter flowers, and warmer loves,
And sing that song again there which
Is dearest, at its proper pitch.
We will sing here, and singing we
Shall hear far off *your* melody
On moonlit summer nights—you ours
Seated among your tropic flowers.

The Realms of Existence as Depicted in the Tibetan Wheel of Life

six sonnets

1. The Realm of the Gods

The gods, throned in their radiant overworld,
Are loath to spare a thought for human care,
But drain the blissful nectar unaware
Of human labours to perdition hurled,
And human lives away in shipwreck whirled,
And human hearts abandoned to despair.
Smiling they sit, as ever young and fair,
With fingers round soft fingers tenderly curled.

But hark! the music of impermanence
From the White Buddha's transcendental lute
Swells in their ears. With gárlands fading fast,
They wring their hands in hapless impotence.
The time has come for tasting other fruit
In other realms. Their glory ends at last.

2. The Realm of the Asuras

"The Tree! the Tree! the Wish-fulfilling Tree!
Tear down its branches! Bear its fruit away!
Fight off the gods, or else we'll lose the day!
Discharge your arrows! Bring up th'artillery!"
Thus shout the anti-gods, as desperately
They strive to conquer in the cosmic fray
With visages distorted, minds astray,
Mad for the prize of immortality.

Sudden amid them shines a fiery sword,
Held in the Verdant Buddha's powerful hand.
It blazes in those faces void of ruth,
Blinding their eyes. They fall back overawed.
Nothing the Sword of Wisdom can withstand.
The noblest warfare is to strive for truth.

3. The Realm of the Hungry Ghosts

With barrel-bellies, mouths like needle-eyes,
And necks as thin as neck of mountain crane,
They seek to feed on what becomes their bane.
Food turns to ordure, pus, or blood—or flies `
Up in their face as flame that never dies.
They feed upon themselves,—arms, legs,—in vain.
They feed upon each other. Oh the pain,
Ravening on that which never satisfies!

Ah drops of mercy! Drops of rare content!
See, the Red Buddha dawns upon their night,
Sprinkling His Nectar from a golden vase—-
The nectarous Message of Enlightenment.
There's no fulfilment in reflected light.
Man's treasure is laid up among the stars.

4. The Realm of the Beings in Hell

Horror and Anguish! Madness and despair!
Weltering in floods of fire, or pinioned fast
In ice, they see a leprous sky o'ercast
With gouts of blood, and suffering everywhere.
One torment worst: amidst the stench and glare,
Within the crystal mirror of the past,—
Mirror of Judgement,—they behold, aghast,
How their own deeds of blood have brought them there.

Yet hope still springs, ev'n in the black abyss.
Purging with flame, with water purifying,
The Smoke-Grey Buddha makes the darkness bright,
Shining a silver cloud. He tells them this:
That from hell's depth there runs, the past defying,
A fearful, narrow pathway to the Light.

5. The Realm of the Animals

The lion, the horse, the elephant, the whale;
Bulls under yoke; rooks noisily debating;
Panthers at play, and goldfish coruscating;
Snake swallowing frog; thrush picking off the snail;
Bird, beast and fish, the female and the male,—
In flocks, in herds, in shoals and schools relating,—
Hunters and hunted,—eating, sleeping, mating,—
Something they lack. By wood, hill, stream, and dale,

The Dark Blue Buddha shows an open book,
Jewel-charactered on leaves of burnished gold.
Behold the treasure of communication,—
Treasure of knowledge,—ne'er to be forsook:
Deeds of great heroes, thoughts of sages old,
Bequeathed to man's remotest generation.

6. The Realm of Men

Grasping the plough, with horse or ox they till
The broad black earth, and having tilled they eat
(Man's honest labour makes his bread more sweet);
They ply the oar; they labour at the mill;
They sing, they dance, carousing with a will
Round festal bonfires; they build towns complete
With walls, towers, temples, markets where they meet;
They shrink from pain, they shrink from death,—until,

Rising in beauty, like the Morning Star,
The Saffron Buddha cries, "Oh have no fear!
Go forth, O mortals! Open is the Door
Of Immortality! Go forth! Here are
The Goal, the Way, the Way-Declarer,—here
Are bowl, robes, ringed staff: you need nothing more."

The Wondering Heart

What can it do, when friends avert
Their eyes, or chose to dwell apart?
What can it do when looks grow cold
That once with love shone bright as gold,
What can it do, the wounded heart?

What can it do, when fairest words
Are changed to foul by devilish art?
What can it do when praises turn
To bitter taunts that scar and burn,
What can it do, the weary heart?

What can it do, when in the midst
Of Truth's own household errors start?
What can it do when from the throne
Of Wisdom folly rules alone,
What can it do, the faithful heart?

What can it do, when all around
The fires of hatred leap and dart?
What can it do when smoke and ash
Await the final thunder-crash,
What can it do, the loving heart?

What can it do, when in the night
A thousand dismal shapes upstart?
What can it do when witches prance
Where shining angel-forms should dance,
What can it do, the wakeful heart?

What can it do, when there are none
To whom it may its griefs impart?
What can it do when on the land
And sea are none that understand,
What can it do, the lonely heart?

What can it do, when oracles
Are dumb, and silence fills the mart?
What can it do when no reply
Comes to it from the earth or sky,
What can it do, the wondering heart?

Yemen Revisited

Flying slower, flying faster,
Birds through a ceiling of alabaster,
Gold against an azure sky,
Trace in bright calligraphy
On those rainbow-bordered pages
Lore sublime of ancient sages,
Wisdom-treasures of the heart
Distilled in words by subtlest art;
Words that through the alabaster
Make the listless heart beat faster,
Till like an enchanted thing
Anon it spreads its golden wing
And seeks to join the happy birds
That on the azure trace those words,
Truth to other eyes revealing
From behind that wondrous ceiling.

Snow-White Revisited

Mirror, mirror on the wall,
Who is the most beautiful of all?

"*You* are most beautiful,"
The mirror always replies,
Else he'd be smashed into pieces
For telling lies.

So he says his piece,
And stays intact.
We're easily flattered,
That's a fact.

We'd as lief hear the truth
As see a ghost.
Mirrors, mirrors on the wall,
Know this better than most.

Truth can appal.

Lovelace Revisited

My mind to me a kingdom is,
Was the gallant poet's song.
Our minds are democracies,
And that's what's wrong.

Every whim has a vote,
Every passion is free to speak.
Our lives are turned upside down,
With a change of government every week.

Sometimes the 'Prime Minister' pleads,
Sometimes tries to be strong,
But take it either way,
He—or she—doesn't last long.

The monarchical principle
Is badly needed, that's plain,
In the mind at least, if it
Is to be a kingdom again.

Lines Composed on Acquiring 'The Works of Samuel Johnson, LL.D.', in Eleven Volumes, MDCCLXXXVII

Three years in earth had Johnson slept,
Three years for him his friends had wept,
When from the presses of the town
Which saw him risen to renown
And in meridian splendour glowing
(Though fear of death was ever growing),
Eleven volumes issued forth
To vindicate his lasting worth,
His learning, piety, and wit,
And wisdom, for most subjects fit,
By Hawkins' diligence compiled
And bound, and stamped, and gilt, and styled
The Works of Samuel Johnson. Grand
In their integrity they stand,
Thrice worthy of the library shelf
Of any man that loves himself
And letters, and humanity,
Even in nineteen eighty-three.
The first set forth the sage's life,
His outward and his inward strife,

His struggles and his victory
("Lord, I commend myself to Thee!")
Over himself. The other ten
Were traced by Johnson's vigorous pen.
(Remembering what the Decad meant
You'll own that ten's no accident.)
Heading them all, three volumes stand,
Lives of the Poets of the land
From Cowley down to studious Gray
And Lyttelton (unread today),
With lives of heroes, scholars' lives,
Where courage dares, and wit contrives.
Decisively he hands them down
The fadeless or the fading crown.
Ramblers and Adventurers follow,
And Idlers too, all far from hollow,
But giving us, in language dense,
Solid truth without pretence
Heightened by rare magnificence
By strong Imagination's aid:
Four volumes to be truly weighed
In none but giant scales—the treasure
Of 'Johnson on Shakespeare' for good measure,
Together with the mighty Plan
Of that on which, a lonely man,
For ten years long he dauntless wrought,
And slowly to completion brought,
Till *Johnson's Dictionary* stood
Foursquare, and trees became a wood.
Next, in one volume marshalled, we
The Statesman and the Traveller see—

And the Apologist of Tea;
The Thinker too, who through a crack
Spied Evil, shuddered, and drew back.
In the last volume of the set
Three well-known characters are met:
The Prince of Abissinia goes
To study men (from boredom's throes
Seeking release), but though long brooded
The *choice of life* is unconcluded;
Tragic Irene meets her fate,
Victim at once of love and hate,
And Theodore his Vision sees.
Thus in their various way do these
Teach us, both whales and little fishes,
The Vanity of Human Wishes.
Now in these dark uncivil days,
Where few indeed can justly praise,
These volumes in my hands I hold,
And though the binding and the gold
Are worn and faded, and the pages
Faintly stained with damp of ages,
In spite of type-face that distresses
The eye with unfamiliar 's's,
Still Johnson's spirit shines as bright
As ever when he saw the light—
Indeed, *our* spirit's lack compounding,
Shines brighter for the gloom surrounding.
Therefore,—although we do not need
The remnants of that savage creed
Which clung to him as Nessus' robe
To Hercules, who'd borne the globe

With less unease, by Pallas aided,—
Because our intellect's degraded
To whim and fancy, and because
We need the strength of wholesome laws
To discipline our wayward hearts
In useful science, joyful arts,
These volumes on the noblest shelf
I place, a blessing to myself
And others, praying they may grant
What men today so badly want,
That bracing "Clear your *mind* of cant."

Alexandrines(?)

'An ineffectual angel', unable to do
Anything very practical, or to follow through
Ideas to the end,—beautiful, soft in the brain,—
'Beating in the void his luminous wings in vain.'

That was Matthew Arnold's well known estimáte
Of Shelley the poet: a pitiful creature, but great.
One would have thought that Matthew, in front of Percy,
Would have fallen on his knees and begged for mercy.

But no, the critic, whether lover or hater,
Invariably trips over the creator.
Creators are stumbling-blocks and stones of offence
To those who are merely pickers up of pence.

Not that Matthew comes in the latter categóry:
He was a poet too—that's another story.
'Mind how you distribute your blessings and curses'
Is the moral of these Alexandrine verses.

(In Racine or Rimbaud, so supple and strong,
Alexandrines elastically bounding along
Are the delight of the French, both the rich and the poor,
But they're not yet acclimatized on England's shore.)

Minerva's Rebuke to Jean Cocteau

My wisdom cold? It was not cold
When amid flames I sprang to light
From Jove's cleft forehead fully armed,
A maiden goddess stern and bright.

It was not cold that day I strove
With blue-haired Neptune on the lea
For Athens of the Violet Crown,
And won her with my olive tree.

Ulysses, Perseus golden-haired,
And many a brother hero bold
Whom I had tutored in their dreams—
They did not find my wisdom cold.

Sleepless am I, nor do I need
The madness of the Bacchic throng
To trace the steps, or sound the note,
For my majestic dance and song.

Whether beneath the Eye of Day,
Or looked on by the Starry Seven,
Around I lead my votaries on
The everlasting roofs of heaven.

I.M., J. and K.

Los and Enitharmon wandered over the graves
Hand in hand, plucking now the nettle now the briar. The sun
Shone on their faces and their limbs were bright with sweat.
'Here let us rest,' said Enitharmon, 'here let us build our bower.
Let us forget the wars of Urthona and the strife of blood,
Forget the flames of inspiration and the terrors of intellect,
Forget Jerusalem, forget Albion and all our brethren, forget
The labours of the furnace and the loom, harp and song.
Let us be all in all to each other, you and I,
Here in a world apart, a Paradise, an Eden, and here
Let us live, drinking each other up, night and day.'

Long Los looked back on the fires of Golgonooza
Flaming against the stars, but at length
Lay down with his head in Enitharmon's lap. She smiled.

Ages passed. The giant forms, covered with snow,
Harden and petrify. The wind howls in the waste.

Before Dawn

Cut off from what I really think and feel,
The substance of my life becomes ideal.

A whited sepulchre, a plaster saint,
Is not much use, however bright its paint.

Dreaming, awake, I must do all I can
To join the inward and the outward man.

Death stares me in the face: I watch and pray.
So near the goal, and yet so far away!

The Priest's Dream

Once more a virgin acolyte he stands
Beside the alter, reverent and demure.
He sees the flutter of white priestly hands:
His head is empty, though his faith is sure.

But now? Awake, slumped in his easy chair
He sees the scattered ash upon his knee,
His greasy cassock—rusty black, threadbare—
And yawns, and wonders if there's fish for tea.

The Gods

One by one the Gods
Of the Underworld emerge
Into the light of day.

Some have raised arms. Some
Bear on their heads
Sun, Moon, horns,
A wide-open lotus flower.

Slowly, gravely, they move,
Emerging from the Underworld
With steady steps,
Walking in procession
Along the curved edge of the world.

Slowly, gravely, they walk,
Descending into the Underworld,
Into the darkness ...

And we must follow.

Resurrection

Osiris is green in colour, dark green.

Long has the embalmed body lain in the tomb,
In the darkness and silence of the stone chamber
Where rows of maidens in black wigs
Walk with lotuses on their heads and lotuses in their cupped hands
For ever and ever round the walls.
Long has the black curled beard pointed at the ceiling, unmoving.
Long have the narrow feet pointed at the ceiling, unmoving.
Long have the fish-eyes stared at the ceiling, unwinking.
Long have the crossed arms grasped flail and sceptre, unyielding.

But now,
Something stirs in the quiet chamber,
Stirs in the darkness.
Shoots, tiny shoots,
Sprout the length of the embalmed body on the painted couch,
Sprouting through the bandages
Like green spears.

Osiris is arisen.

Haiku

Thrown on the white wall
Shadows of flowers
Have nothing to say.

The Sunflower's Farewell

Aloft on its tall stalk the sunflower hangs
As though half weary. Harvest long since reaped,
It sees beyond the ivied crumbling wall
Blue-vaulted stubble in faint sunlight steeped.

Aloft on its dry stalk the sunflower hangs
In silence: in the West, the round red sun.
The yellow petals, once its glory, wilt:
Its seed is ready and its work is done.

Index of First Lines